RACING AND LURE COURSING
DOGS

BY MARIE-THERESE MILLER, PH.D.

CANINE

★

ATHLETES

SportsZone

An Imprint of Abdo Publishing
abdobooks.com

abdobooks.com

Published by Abdo Publishing, a division of ABDO, PO Box 398166, Minneapolis, Minnesota 55439. Copyright © 2019 by Abdo Consulting Group, Inc. International copyrights reserved in all countries. No part of this book may be reproduced in any form without written permission from the publisher. SportsZone™ is a trademark and logo of Abdo Publishing.

Printed in the United States of America, North Mankato, Minnesota
092018
012019

Cover Photo: Shutterstock Images
Interior Photos: Henri Faure/Shutterstock Images, 5; Shutterstock Images, 7, 17; Julian Maldonado/Shutterstock Images, 9; Grigorita Ko/Shutterstock Images, 11 (top), 20; Liliya Kulianionak/Shutterstock Images, 11 (bottom); iStockphoto, 13, 23; Olga Gorovenko/Shutterstock Images, 19; Milan Vachal/Shutterstock Images, 24; Naturfoto-Online/Alamy, 28

Editor: Marie Pearson
Series Designer: Craig Hinton

Library of Congress Control Number: 2018949088

Publisher's Cataloging-in-Publication Data

Names: Miller, Marie-Therese, author.
Title: Racing and lure coursing dogs / by Marie-Therese Miller.
Description: Minneapolis, Minnesota : Abdo Publishing, 2019 | Series: Canine athletes | Includes online resources and index.
Identifiers: ISBN 9781532117404 (lib. bdg.) | ISBN 9781641855976 (pbk) | ISBN 9781532170263 (ebook)
Subjects: LCSH: Dog sports--Juvenile literature. | Dog racing--Juvenile literature. | Dogs--Behavior--Juvenile literature.
Classification: DDC 798.8--dc23

TABLE OF
CONTENTS

HUNTING TURNED TO SPORT

The sun is warm on the large grassy field. Three whippets, each wearing a yellow, pink, or blue blanket, stand at the lure coursing start line. They strain against their slip leads and bark. They are excited to chase the lure, a white plastic bag on a motorized string. The huntmaster asks the handlers if they are ready. They answer, "Yes," and the huntmaster calls, "Tallyho!" The handlers quickly release their dogs.

The whippets race after the lure. They gallop along straight sections of the course and perform difficult turns,

Whippets make speedy lure coursing dogs.

all while following their "prey," the lure. The lure's motor whirrs. A judge watches from close by, writing notes about the dogs' coursing skills and giving them scores. The dog that scores highest in certain areas, such as speed and following the lure, wins.

Less than a minute later, the course is over. The dogs catch and play with the lure for a moment as a reward for a good chase. The handlers cheer for the dogs. The huntmaster calls, "Retrieve the hounds!" and the handlers place their dogs back on leashes. The next dogs get ready for their course.

ACCEPTED LURE COURSING BREEDS

The American Sighthound Field Association (ASFA) recognizes the following breeds: Afghan hound, Azawakh, basenji, borzoi, cirneco dell'Etna, greyhound, Ibizan hound, Irish wolfhound, Italian greyhound, pharaoh hound, Rhodesian ridgeback, saluki, silken windhound, Scottish deerhound, sloughi, and whippet.

The American Kennel Club (AKC) recognizes all those breeds except the silken windhound. The AKC additionally recognizes the Portuguese podengo pequeno. For certain awards, the AKC allows these Foundation Stock Service Breeds to compete: Azawakh, Norrbottenspets, Peruvian Inca orchid, Portuguese podengo medio and grande, and Thai ridgeback.

6

Racing takes place on a formal track. There are no sharp turns as there are in coursing.

COURSING AND RACING

Lure coursing is one of two sports designed for sighthounds. The other sport is racing, in which dogs chase a lure on a flat track in either a straight line or an oval curve. Sighthounds tend to use their eyesight to hunt other animals, their prey. They are talented at seeing things that move and are far away. Many hunting dogs use their excellent sense of smell to find prey, but sighthounds usually focus on what they can see.

AMAZING SIGHTHOUNDS

Before firearms existed, people bred sighthounds to help them hunt. These types of dogs have been hunters' companions for a long time. Artwork of dogs that resembles salukis and greyhounds has been found on pottery from 5000 BCE.

The hunters bred sighthounds with bodies that could handle the prey, terrain, and weather in their particular area of the world. Borzois, for example, were bred to hunt wolves in Russia. They are large dogs that can tangle with wolves, and they have long fur to handle the cold

While coursing hares for sport is illegal in the United States and generally considered inhumane, it is allowed in other countries.

Russian winters. Salukis were gazelle hunters in the desert, so they had to have speed and endurance. Their bodies can withstand the desert heat.

Sighthounds have amazing physical traits that make them well suited for their hunting jobs. They are often light boned and muscular, with slender legs, heads, and muzzles. They have long, thin necks. Their lean shape lets them run with less wind resistance, and their long necks allow them to reach for prey.

Sighthounds also have deep chests with plenty of room for their lungs to expand and take in oxygen and for their hearts to beat as they run. They leave the ground twice with each gallop. Their hind legs push them totally off the ground, then their forelegs do the same. This is known as a double-suspension gallop, which makes their running powerful and fast. It is the same gallop that gives the cheetah its speed. Greyhounds can run as fast as 40 miles per hour (64 km/h).

Sighthounds' eyes see movement well and can detect prey as far away as half a mile (0.8 km). They have a better

DOUBLE-SUSPENSION
GALLOP

ALL FOUR FEET OFF THE GROUND
UNDERNEATH THE DOG

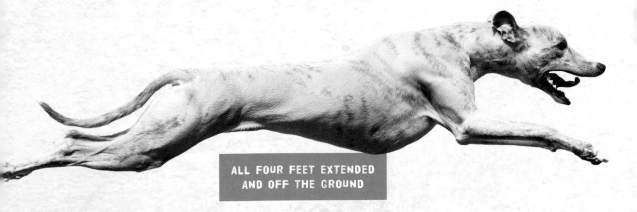

ALL FOUR FEET EXTENDED
AND OFF THE GROUND

field of vision than humans do. Sighthounds have up to 270-degree field of vision, while humans have 180-degree field of vision. This also helps sighthounds find prey.

Sighthound owners in the United States used to test their dogs' instincts with open field trials, where the dogs chased live jackrabbits. But many dogs were hurt when they got tangled in barbed wire fences. Racing began in the early 1900s in the United States. Owen Patrick Smith invented an artificial lure system and began professional greyhound racing on an oval track. It was safer than chasing live prey. The National Oval Track Racing Association (NOTRA) was formed in 1992 for amateur sighthounds to participate in oval track racing. In 1995 the Large Gazehound Racing Association (LGRA) was founded for amateur straight track racing.

Lyle Gillette and his friends started lure coursing in the early 1970s. It was more like chasing live prey. In 1972 Gillette began the American Sighthound Field Association (ASFA). The ASFA offers lure-coursing trials across the United States. Later, the American Kennel Club (AKC) began holding lure-coursing trials as well.

Sometimes owners have their puppies watch adults course to teach them to get excited to run.

CHOOSING AND CONDITIONING SIGHTHOUNDS

Those who are interested in competing in lure coursing or racing should select a sighthound breed with the best temperament for the household. Research breeds to find the best fit, then find a responsible breeder. Ask whether the puppy's parents hold coursing or racing titles. If so, the pup has a good chance of becoming a canine athlete as well.

To raise a well-behaved puppy, the pup needs some basic obedience training. Socialize the pup by getting it used to all sorts of people, animals, and situations. Take the puppy to coursing and racing events so the pup is petted and handled by many people and interacts with other dogs. It is good for the pup to see the lure and feel different textures under its paws. This helps make the puppy confident.

Sighthounds need a quality dog food. They should not be overfed, as extra weight strains the joints. The pup should get exercise. Growing pups' joints are easily injured, so exercise should not be too strenuous. Daily walks and romps through a field are excellent options. Adult dogs can jog on a leash alongside a bike.

To ready a puppy to chase a lure, many people attach a plastic bag to a lunge whip. They make a game of letting the puppy chase the bag. Between four and six months old, the pup can run short straight tracks, which is good practice for lure coursing and racing.

For racing, the pup needs to practice being in the starting box. This box is a row of slots, one for each dog. It is designed so that all the slot doors open at the same time so the dogs get a fair start. Let the pup adjust to the box step by step. The first lessons have the pup walk through an open starting box. The last lessons have the puppy in a closed starting box and adjusting to the front door flipping open. Racing puppies also have to learn to wear a muzzle. Put a bit of peanut butter inside the muzzle before placing it on the pup. Or put the muzzle on before a meal. This way, the pup connects wearing the muzzle with a positive treat.

Just like a human athlete, the dog needs a warm-up walk before a course. This makes the muscles flexible and therefore less prone to injury. After the course, cool the dog down with another walk until the dog stops panting. Bring plenty of water to keep the dog hydrated and find a shady spot to keep the hound cool. On hot days, handlers might spray the dogs with water to fight the heat.

CANINE ATHLETE CARE

Karen Peterson, owner of the No. 7 ASFA Rhodesian ridgeback lure courser in the country in 2017, keeps her dog athletes in top shape. She has a knowledgeable veterinarian, chiropractor, and massage therapist for her dogs. Physical therapists also work with canine athletes to keep them in superb condition for the sport and to help them recover from illnesses or injuries. Physical therapists might do certain stretches with the dog, have the dog swim in a pool to help its heart and lungs work better, or place the dog on a floating board to improve balance and make limb and core muscles stronger.

LURE COURSING FUN

In lure coursing, dogs compete on an open grass field. ASFA courses must be more than 500 yards (460 m) long. AKC courses must be more than 600 yards (550 m), as long as five football fields.

The lure is made of a white plastic bag. It is attached to a string pulled by a motor. Pulleys are staked into the ground at certain spots on the field. Then the string is placed around the pulleys. The lure on the string goes in straight lines and makes turns around the pulleys,

Even the small Italian greyhound enjoys catching the lure.

mimicking a hare or rabbit's movements when chased in the wild. The lure is even called a bunny.

The person who works the lure is called the lure operator. The lure operator often stands on a ladder for a good view of the dogs. He or she keeps the lure 10 to 30 yards (9–27 m) in front of the hounds. The operator makes sure that the dogs do not catch the lure during the course and that the hounds do not get tangled in the string.

The dogs that compete in lure coursing trials must be at least one year old. Younger dogs are still growing, and their joints could be hurt making sharp turns. The dogs need to be purebred sighthounds. They race in groups of two, called braces, or in groups of three, called trios. Dogs usually perform better when other dogs run with them.

It is hard for the judges to tell dogs apart when the dogs are moving so fast so far away. That is why the dogs wear colored vests, known as blankets. These bright colors make it easier for the judge to know which dog is which when giving them points.

Two pharaoh hounds chase after the lure.

Each dog also wears a slip lead. The slip lead has a wide, padded collar with metal rings on both ends. The leash loops through the metal rings. The slip lead is made so the handlers can release their hounds easily and quickly. At the start line, the handlers release the slip leads at the tallyho, the lead slips away from the dogs' necks, and the dogs race after the lure. If any one of the dogs begins before the *T* sound of the tallyho, the dog can lose points. At the end of the course, the handlers leash their dogs. The dog can lose points if this takes too long.

During the course, the judge stands directly on the field to keep a close eye on the dogs. The judge gives each dog points for certain skills. Both the ASFA and AKC award points for speed, agility, endurance, and follow. Follow means how close the dogs stay to the lure. However, follow is tricky to judge. It is important to understand the

Rhodesian ridgebacks are stockier than most sighthounds, but they still love the chase.

way each breed hunts. Rhodesian ridgebacks and borzois, for example, were bred to hunt in groups. During a course, one ridgeback might follow the lead for a while then let another ridgeback take over. On the other hand, breeds such as greyhounds and whippets follow the lure closely.

The ASFA has another score for enthusiasm, while the AKC scores overall ability. The point total a dog can earn on an ASFA course is 100, and the AKC total is 50.

In lure coursing, dogs compete for ribbons, rosettes, and titles. Titles are awarded for athletic achievements and are indicated by letters that go before or after a dog's name. They get these awards by competing in various stakes. The open stake is for any sighthound that is a qualified courser. To become a qualified courser, the dog runs a course with another of the same breed. A judge then certifies that the dog finished the course and did not interfere with the other dog. There is a stake just for dogs with the field champion title, and one known as the veteran stake for older dogs. Depending on the breed, the dogs are veterans beginning at five, six, or seven years old.

During the stake, the dogs run with their own breed. All dogs run two courses: a preliminary and a final. The direction of the lure is reversed during the final to keep challenging the dogs. The high-scoring dogs in a breed compete for Best of Breed. Finally, the Best of Breed dogs compete for Best in Field. Some lure coursing events also hold a singles stake, in which the hounds run a course alone. These hounds cannot try for Best of Breed or Best in Field.

PORTUGUESE PODENGO PEQUENO

The AKC recognizes the Portuguese podengo pequeno as a hound and allows the breed to lure course. However, as requested by the parent club specializing in this breed, the AKC does not allow them to compete against other breeds for Best in Field. This breed is so small that the handlers are concerned it might get bumped or mistaken for prey when coursing with larger breeds.

CHAPTER 4

THE RACING DOG

The Large Gazehound Racing Association (LGRA) organizes straight track racing for sighthounds that are at least one year old. The purebred sighthounds are largely the same breeds that the ASFA allows, but without whippets. At the beginning of a straight track race, the handlers place the hounds in a starting box. The starting box has a line of dog-sized cubbies with a number on the front of each one. When the race starts, the front of the starting box flips open and frees the dogs to run. Some of the larger dogs, such as Irish wolfhounds, might not fit in the starting box. Their handlers can release those hounds

A saluki reaches for the lure at the end of a race.

Borzois break from the starting box.

by hand slipping them. In a straight track race, the dogs run 200 yards (180 m) on a track with no turns.

The dogs race against their own breed. The dogs are also grouped by their racing skills, which is calculated by how well they ran in previous races. They run three times in a day with, at most, four dogs in each race.

The dog whose nose crosses the finish line first is placed first and scores the most points, the second dog is awarded second place with fewer points, and so on. At the end of the day, awards are given for each breed, such as the highest-scoring hound or the five top racers. Even the slowest dog may win a prize, usually a stuffed turtle toy. Over time, the dogs can earn titles with their points, such as Gazehound Racing Champion (GRC).

The lure that the dogs chase in straight racing is a drag lure. It goes in only one direction from the start to the finish line. At the beginning of each race, someone has to bring the lure back to the start. Many clubs use an all-terrain vehicle for this. The lure might be made of fur or fake fur with a noisemaker inside, which is called a squawker. With every bounce along the ground, the squawker squeaks. Both the sound and the movement of the lure excite the dogs to the chase.

Racing dogs wear different colored blankets with numbers that match the dogs' starting box number. The dogs also wear collars so they can be quickly leashed at the race's end. Because a straight track race starts and ends in different places, one person starts the dog and another retrieves it.

The dogs also wear muzzles over their snouts for racing. The muzzle has to be loose enough for them to pant. Muzzles keep the dogs from biting the lure at the end of the race or being aggressive with the other dogs. It also makes the dog's nose easier to see when the judges need to decide the placement of dogs at the finish line.

Racing uses several judges. Foul judges stand along the track, often at the start, middle, and end. They watch and decide if any dog is acting aggressively toward or interfering with the other dogs running. A dog that commits a foul is disqualified from the race. At least two finish line judges are on either end of the finish line to decide the placement of the hounds. More than two judges are often needed for competitive races, such as with greyhounds, because the finish for these quick racers is often a close call.

WHIPPET RACING

LGRA does not include whippets in its straight track events. Whippets have their own organizations for racing, such as the Whippet Racing Association. The racing rules are similar, but six whippets can race at a time.

OVAL TRACK

Sighthounds at least one year old can race around an oval or U-shaped track in events held by the National Oval Track Racing Association (NOTRA). NOTRA mostly includes the same sighthounds as LGRA, with the addition of the Portuguese podengos and whippets. The track length is between 241 yards (220 m) and 440 yards (403 m). Oval track racing rules are similar to those in straight track racing. However, four races, known as programs, can be run in a day of oval racing, and whippets are allowed to run in groups of five dogs. Because the dogs run all the way around in oval track racing, the handlers can start and retrieve their own hounds. With NOTRA points, the hounds can earn titles, such as Oval Racing Championship (ORC).

Most people who participate in racing do it as a hobby. They don't typically win prize money, and they have only a few dogs. But professional greyhound racing, in which the participating dogs can win money and spectators bet on the dogs, can be found in some states, such as Alabama and Florida. Racing greyhounds are kept in kennels near or at racetracks. They are released from their kennels several

 Afghan hounds race around the bend on an oval track.

times a day for exercise and to play with other greyhounds
in large, fenced-in fields. Racing greyhounds are typically
well cared for because an unfit or abused dog will not win
races. But some people are concerned about the dogs'
risk of injury during races and what happens to the dogs
after they can no longer race. In the past, many racing
greyhounds were killed when they were no longer useful.
In 1987 the American Greyhound Council was organized
to oversee the welfare of greyhounds. Today, 90 percent

of retired greyhounds in the United States are now adopted as pets or used to breed future racers. However, a number of greyhounds that cannot be adopted or used in breeding programs continue to be killed.

Hounds running oval track have to be smart about their position while racing. Clever dogs move quickly to the inside of the track, called the rail, so they do not have as far to run and can travel the track faster. While running the curves, the dogs have to be agile and know how to control their speed. These racing strategies make oval racing thrilling to watch.

Participating in competitive lure coursing or racing is great fun for both the handler and hound. But win or lose, the handler still goes home with a dog to love.

GLOSSARY

agile
Able to move easily or gracefully.

bet
To gamble money on something, such as the outcome of a race.

chiropractor
A health-care professional who treats the musculoskeletal system, particularly the back and neck.

disqualified
Not permitted to take part in the coursing or racing event.

endurance
The ability to do something for a long time without becoming tired.

field of vision
Everything that can be seen without turning the head.

lunge whip
A long training stick often used with horses.

muzzle
A covering worn over the dog's snout to prevent biting.

parent club
An organization that represents a certain breed of dog.

pulley
A small wheel with a groove in which a string can rest; it spins as the string is pulled through.

responsible
Known for making good decisions; trustworthy.

temperament
The dog's disposition or personality. Each dog has its own temperament: some are gentle and relaxed, and some are energetic and playful.

MORE INFORMATION

ONLINE RESOURCES

To learn more about racing and lure coursing dogs, visit **abdobooklinks.com**. These links are routinely monitored and updated to provide the most current information available.

BOOKS

Furstinger, Nancy. *Dogs*. Minneapolis, MN: Abdo Publishing, 2014.

Hamilton, S. L. *Dogs*. Minneapolis, MN: Abdo Publishing, 2014.

Sundance, Kyra. *101 Dog Tricks, Kids Edition: Fun and Easy Activities, Games, and Crafts*. Beverly, MA: Quarry, 2014.

INDEX

ABOUT THE AUTHOR

Marie-Therese Miller writes nonfiction books for children and young adults. She is the author of *Managing Responsibilities*, *Rachel Carson*, and several dog books. Her stories have appeared in nearly a dozen *Chicken Soup for the Soul* books. Miller earned her Ph.D. in English from St. John's University. She and her husband have five children and live in New York's Hudson Valley.